A Guide for Writers and Authors

SYLVIA A. COLE

The Purpose of this Guide

Do you have a life-changing story or testimony that will impact the lives of others? Are you ready to share your story with the world but don't know where to begin? If so, this guide is for YOU! It is designed to give you a blueprint and help guide you through the process of writing. Writing a book can be a difficult and challenging undertaking that requires resilience and consistency. It is also liberating, therapeutic, humbling and rewarding, particularly if conducted in a manageable fashion. I shall never forget the pride I felt when I received the press proof of my first book in the mail, which was a culmination of my hard work and resilience. Also, your book may provide you with additional income, showcase your expertise in your field, and even give you access to a new audience. It is also quite possible you will write a book that that will impact the lives of thousands and perhaps millions in a way they have never known. There is nothing like someone approaching you at a conference and saying, "Your book changed my life" or "Your book gave me hope when I lost my brother." It is my hope this guide will push you to just start writing!

Table of Contents

Your Story is a Message

Everybody goes through things in life that they may not

always be proud of or happy about.

There are moments where we suffer and struggle and

wonder, "Why me?" It is in the thick of our storm

where our story is often formed.

Our story begins the moment we face challenges

that are often life-changing. When we see and experience the

victory, that is the message that is meant to be shared.

Use your words to inspire, encourage and empower others!

Your story happened IN you and FOR you to share with

and bring hope to others!

Your Story is Your Message

Identify Your Target Audience

It is crucial to make sure there is an audience for your book, because you definitely want people to read it. People may need your book, but will they actually want it or even purchase it? When you identify your audience prior to writing, you will be able to keep the focus on your message throughout the writing process. As a writer, it is constantly in my mind as I write each sentence or chapter, who am I writing this book for? This also helps to keep you focused on being an impact. Throughout our lives, we engage in the process of audience targeting. I fondly recall when my nieces and nephews were young children, they knew I was the aunt who would give them whatever they wanted. They identified me early on as their target audience of one. However, we target our audience by building relationships which are necessary in every aspect of our lives. It is often stated, "Everybody needs somebody."

You must bear in mind that your book is not for everyone, although you may have written a great story. No one can be pleased in every situation and knowing your audience will also be an asset when you begin the promotional phase for your book.

As a writer, you are writing to impact someone else's life or solve a problem. Also, targeting your audience will result in more fans and followers. Once you have written a book, these same fans/followers will look forward to your next project.

Also, what is the genre of your book? Make sure the category you choose for your book will actually reach your target audience by having it in the appropriate genre.

However, do not just limit your book to your primary audience. There are also secondary markets like school districts, organizations, and institutions. For example, if you are writing a book about self-esteem, the school district would be an excellent secondary market because they can recommend this book to parents as well. There are endless possibilities so don't limit yourself.

Know what is special about YOUR book and develop a hook to reel them in.

Where to Begin Your Writing Journey

Writing starts with what is ALL in your head! It is also vital that your head is straight prior to beginning. You must be self-confident and believe that you have a voice and can write and potentially be an expert in your field or achieve your writing goal. Each of us has a story that has the potential to affect someone else's life. You must think positive thoughts. Devise a list of positive daily confessions such as:

1. "I can do all things through Christ who strengthens me" (Philippians 4:6).

2. I have a story that will impact the lives of others.

3. I have time to write each day.

4. I refuse to be distracted.

5. My story will be a part of my legacy.

6. I will review my writing goals daily.

7. I will establish myself as an authority in my field.

8. I am passionate about my writing.

9. I am resilient and can handle any challenge.

10. I will become a published author this year.

This includes your thoughts, memories, and random words. When you start the writing process, you will want to write about all that comes to your mind. Do not worry if things do not make sense. You will be able to narrow it down later.

Use the space below to write out your thoughts.

_____

_____

_____

_____

_____

_____

_____

_____

Pre-Writing

This step requires that you create an outline of everything you desire to talk about in your book and also come up with relevant ideas and stories you may want to share. All of us experience some type of adversity at some point in our lives. We also exhibit amazing resilience which allows us to bounce back or get back to our normal. Sharing your story allows you to own the story as well as helps and encourages others. You have a voice. I recently heard someone say, "No one can say what you have to say in the way that only you can say it." The key is that you must believe that this is indeed the case.

Hence, you should begin by completing a rough draft outline of your book. You will then use this outline to make a rough draft of your entire table of contents which includes your book chapters and sub-chapters. Proceed by adding a few sentences to each chapter to validate the points you wish to make. Stories are powerful, easy to remember, and will resonate with the reader. Also, readers want to know you and the story behind what you are sharing. Review your outline to ensure you have not omitted anything. You may also want to review similar books to see what they may have covered. You must then make sure your outline is flowing and you move from one point to another in a seamless fashion. Make whatever necessary changes are needed at the time.

The Story Build-Out

Many people who start writing think writing the outline is a waste of time. However, your outline is the MOST important part of your writing journey and CANNOT be left out. Use this guide to help you write your outline to compose your story.

*Themes

What is the focus of your Story?

*The Take Away

What lesson do you want people to learn and take away from your story?

*Use Your Voice

What kind of writer are you?

(Descriptive, Passionate, Inspirational, Suspenseful, Mystery)

*Your Book Title: Subtitle (If Applicable)

Write the name of your Book!

Your Outline

Your chapter should include the title of the chapter and at least three points you will discuss in detail within the chapter.

Chapter 1

_____

Points:

1._____

2._____

3._____

Chapter 2

_____

Points:

1._____

2._____

3._____

Chapter 3

_____

Points:

1._____

2._____

3._____

Chapter 4

_____

Points:

1._____

2._____

3._____

Chapter 5

_____

Points:

1._____

2._____

3._____

Drafting

During the process of drafting, you must avoid editing and making revisions. At this stage, your primary goal is to get your story written down or typed in its entirety. As you refer to your already written outline, initiating the writing process should be done with ease. It matters not what you have written at this point. Remember: Write now and edit later.

Another significant point is to determine the length of your book. The strategy I used was to find a book about the same size and number of pages that closely mirrored what I desired my final book to look like. You should count the number of chapters, number of pages in each chapter, and the number of words. This will give you an idea of how long each chapter should be and the number of chapters your book should include. Also, when typing in a Word document, you will be able to see the number of typed pages and word count.

WHAT to SAY and WHEN

When telling your story, one key thing to remember is that you

CANNOT TELL EVERYTHING!

I know the urge to "TELL IT ALL" can be very tempting. However,

you have to look for the moments in your life that:

1. Had the MOST impact

2. Where you learned an ENORMOUS Lesson

3. You faced a GIGANTIC Challenge

4. You overcame an INSURMOUNTABLE obstacle

5. You experienced the GREATEST joy

How to tell your story...

1. Make use of the themes within your book and pick themes that are compelling and will grab the attention of the reader.

2. Highlight the moments of the stories that had the most impact, such as when it was the toughest and give your reader a clear walk of that moment.

3. Take the time to BE IN the story as you are telling it. You will face a lot of emotions as you are writing, but this is good! I am hopeful and encouraged as I write. When you feel what your readers feel, that is how you know they will get what you desire!

REVISION

This step allows you to go back and edit all of your work. You may have portions that may need to be removed or even switched to another chapter. You may also want to add stories you may not have previously thought about as well as create additional chapters. I know from experience that this step will require and should require several revisions as you want to release the best product possible.

PROOFREADING and EDITING

My advice regarding proofreading and editing is to hire someone, if at all possible. No one wants to read a book with a ton of mistakes. It is very easy to miss errors and typos if you are anxious about getting your book released as soon as possible. A professional editor will be able to fix the quality of your entire book and correct any errors as well.

It is possible you may not be able to hire a professional and can ask a few friends or family members who are not judgmental to assist you. Remind them you are not asking them to write your story, just point out any grammatical errors and typos. Another strategy would be to ask a college English professor to proof and edit your book. Lastly, use the buddy system. A fellow writer can review your book and you review theirs.

FORMATTING

Many times we have heard others say or we may have even made the following statement, "Don't judge a book by its cover." However, I must admit that an attractive cover is appealing and arouses curiosity about a particular book. There are many factors or steps that should be undertaken when formatting your book. These include the following:

1.   Proofreading (discussed in previous chapter)

2.   Reviewing already published books

3.   Establishing your book format

4.   Fonts and Tabs

5.   Chapter Titles and Subheads

6.   Headers, Footers, and Page Numbers

7.   Illustrations

8.   Front Cover

9. Back Cover

10. You are not finished Yet!

SELF-PUBLISHING

Over the past few years I have researched, absorbed, and utilized a ton of information while self-publishing three books. You might ask, what is self-publishing? As defined in numerous literature, self-publishing refers to "the process by which you write and publish a book without the involvement of an agent or traditional publishing house." In other words, the author is totally responsible for production, publishing, marketing and book sales.

One of the great benefits of self-publishing a book is you maintain control, input, and output. A self-published book also has the potential to exist forever and consistently earn the author income as opposed to traditional publishing in which a book may be discontinued due to lack of sales. Self-published authors should write and write and continue to grow their brand.

Obviously, the disadvantage of self-publishing can be that the author has to do everything. I must admit—initially it was overwhelming and exhausting but I learned a great deal throughout the process. My labor was not in vain and I am now a three-time published author and continuing to write.

Decide how you are going to sell your book—print or digital, or perhaps both. CreatSpace is a great company to use for print on demand. Write an eye-catching description and also design an appealing book cover. Put your book on the platforms you choose for sales and remember, YOU are responsible for marketing. Lastly, don't forget to keep writing!

INSPIRATIONAL QUOTES

"I can do all things through Christ who strengthens me" (Philippians 4:6).

"If I waited till I felt like writing, I'd never write at all" (Anne Tyler).

"There is nothing to writing. All you do is sit down at a typewriter and bleed" (Ernest Hemingway).

"Either write something worth reading or do something worth writing" (Benjamin Franklin).

"No one can tell your story so tell it yourself. No one can write your story so write it yourself" (Unknown).

"The secret to being a writer is not to expect others to value what you've done as you value it. Do not expect anyone else to perceive in it the emotions you have invested in it. Once this is understood, all will be well" (Joyce Carol Oates).

"Excuses stand between you and divine creativity" (I.V. Hilliard).

"If a story is in you, it has to come out" (William Faulkner).

"A professional writer is an amateur who never quit" (Richard Bach).

"Being a good writer is not about nailing it the first time. It's about not giving up until a piece is finished" (Unknown)

"Write like it matters and it will" (Libba Bay).

"Writing is a calling, not a choice" (Isabel Allendo).

"Have God make a message out of your mess" (Joyce Meyer).

"Start writing no matter what. The water does not flow until the faucet is turned on" (Louis L'Amour).

"Write what disturbs you, what you fear, what you have not been willing to speak about. Be willing to be split open" (Natalie Goldberg).

"There is a winner in you. You were created to be successful, to accomplish your goal, to leave your mark on this generation. You have greatness in you" (Joel Osteen).

"Your dreams don't stop being dreams because of circumstances. The secret of becoming a writer is to write, write, and keep on writing" (Ken MacLeod).

"Don't forget—no one else sees the world the way you do, so no one else can tell the stories that you have to tell" (Charles de Lint).

"Others can inspire you, but ultimately the only thing that empowers you is what lies within you and learning how to better utilize what you have been given" (T.D. Jakes).

"Each new day presents another opportunity to write. Rejoice and keep on writing" (Sylvia A. Cole).

To Contact the AUTHOR

Email: called2writeclub@gmail.com

About the AUTHOR

Sylvia A. Cole is an author, educator, speaker, and writing coach. She is passionate about writing, teaching, and speaking and has a desire to see others impact the world and leave a legacy that will be read and remembered by generations to come. She is also the founder of CALLED 2 Write Writing Services which offers writing coaching, editing, and consulting services. As a writing coach, her mission is to encourage and empower others to share their testimony or story while providing support and guidance. This encourager and prayer warrior is also the author of the following books: I TAKE GOD AT HIS WORD and LAY ASIDE YOUR WEIGHT AND REST: FINDING PEACE WHEN YOUR BURDENS SEEM MORE THAN YOU CAN BEAR.